# INSIDE LAW ENFORCEMENT

# INSIDE THE CIA

Bridey Heing

Enslow Publishing
101 W. 23rd Street
Suite 240
New York, NY 10011
USA

enslow.com

Published in 2020 by Enslow Publishing, LLC.
101 W. 23rd Street, Suite 240, New York, NY 10011

Copyright © 2020 by Enslow Publishing, LLC.

All rights reserved.

No part of this book may be reproduced by any means without the written permission of the publisher.

### Library of Congress Cataloging-in-Publication Data

Names: Heing, Bridey, author.
Title: Inside the CIA / Bridey Heing.
Description: New York : Enslow Publishing, 2020. | Series: Inside law enforcement | Includes bibliographical references and index. | Audience: Grades: 5-8.
Identifiers: LCCN 2018058100| ISBN 9781978507388 (library bound) | ISBN 9781978508514 (pbk.)
Subjects:  LCSH: United States. Central Intelligence Agency—Juvenile literature.
Classification: LCC JK468.I6 H475 2020 | DDC 327.1273—dc23
LC record available at https://lccn.loc.gov/2018058100

Printed in the United States of America

**To Our Readers:** We have done our best to make sure all website addresses in this book were active and appropriate when we went to press. However, the author and the publisher have no control over and assume no liability for the material available on those websites or on any websites they may link to. Any comments or suggestions can be sent by email to customerservice@enslow.com.

**Photo Credits:** Cover, pp. 1, 41 Mark Wilson/Getty Images; p. 5 Glowimages/Getty Images; p. 8 Fox Photos/Hulton Archive/Getty Images; p. 11 Bettmann/Getty Images; p. 15 Gorodenkoff/Shutterstock.com; p. 16 Motortion Films/Shutterstock.com; p. 20 Pe3k/Shutterstock.com; p. 23 Stephen Jaffe/AFP/Getty Images; p. 24 John Macdougall/AFP/Getty Images; p. 28 Harry Langdon/Archive Photos/Getty Images; p. 31 © AP Images; p. 35 Paul J. Richards/Getty Images; p. 36 Iurii Chornysh/Shutterstock.com; p. 38 Chip Somodevilla/Getty Images; p. 40 Alexander Weickart/Shutterstock.com.

# CONTENTS

Introduction ................................................................. 4

**Chapter 1**  A History of the CIA ............................... 7

**Chapter 2**  The Duties of the CIA .......................... 14

**Chapter 3**  The CIA Overseas ................................. 22

**Chapter 4**  Controversies of the CIA ..................... 30

**Chapter 5**  The Future of the CIA .......................... 37

Chapter Notes ............................................................ 43

Glossary ..................................................................... 44

Further Reading ........................................................ 46

Index .......................................................................... 47

# INTRODUCTION

Founded in the aftermath of World War II, the Central Intelligence Agency (CIA) has since become a cornerstone of US intelligence gathering in just over half a century and an agency with global reach. But it has also become embroiled in some of the twentieth and twenty-first centuries' most significant foreign policy controversies, in part due to tactics that many countries feel are invasive and unethical. The story of the CIA is in many ways the story of the United States—a country that emerged from World War II with significantly more power and has since struggled to balance international interests with ethical obligation.

The CIA started as the Office of Strategic Services (OSS), an agency founded in 1942 during World War II by President Franklin Roosevelt. Prior to the founding of OSS, intelligence gathering had been conducted by the branches of the military and the Federal Bureau of Investigation (FBI); however, there was no coordination or centralization of that process or the resulting information. OSS didn't take over these duties from the various departments that already oversaw them, but rather carried out its own intelligence gathering, oversaw espionage and activities behind enemy lines, and assisted with propaganda and post-war planning. It was meant to provide guidance to the Joint Chiefs of Staff, helping them in the effort to beat the Axis powers.

Following the war, the OSS was disbanded and the CIA was established. Sometimes simply called the Agency, the CIA became the primary

The Central Intelligence Agency is famous for its spies and covert operations, but as a law enforcement agency, it is responsible for the safety of Americans around the world.

agency through which intelligence traveled and was analyzed. It served a critical function as the Cold War challenged conventional warfare and the United States became the leading global superpower. But the CIA also took on more sinister plotting, taking part in coups around the world and engaging in practices like enhanced interrogation, including modes of torture sanctioned by the government. This sense of the CIA as a threat alongside being a resource has grown in recent years, due to scrutiny of its lack of transparency.

The CIA has been an integral, if often little understood, player on the world stage since the middle of the twentieth century. How does an agency founded so recently become a leading force for change and intelligence gathering around the world? And how does that story explain the part the CIA plays in law enforcement? This book will look at how the CIA was developed, the role it plays in law enforcement, and what the future might hold for this storied agency.

CHAPTER 1

# A HISTORY OF THE CIA

The CIA was founded in 1947, but the story of the agency doesn't start there. It begins in 1942, with the establishment of the Office of Strategic Services, an agency that was intended to help the United States and other Allied countries fight the Axis powers of World War II. After the war, the OSS became the CIA, which took on an ever-growing role in shaping US policy and interests in the international space. This is especially true in the context of the Cold War, when spies and double agents became political tools as much as cultural forces.

## Office of Strategic Services

When World War II began, the United States' intelligence efforts were disorganized and had little coordination between agencies and departments. Anti-espionage efforts, code breaking, and general collection of information were divided among multiple organizations. The military

The CIA was formed during World War II as a response to the Japanese bombing of Pearl Harbor and the lack of a central intelligence-gathering operation in the United States.

conducted some collection and analysis overseas, while the FBI handled domestic efforts. But these efforts were largely insufficient, with little effective oversight to ensure all information was handled as well as possible. One senior diplomat, Robert Murphy, said, "It must be confessed that our intelligence organization in 1940 was primitive and inadequate. It was timid…"[1]

The "timid" nature of intelligence gathering and analyzing efforts became a major threat to security as the United State entered World War II in December 1941, following the Japanese attack on Pearl Harbor in Hawaii. President Franklin Roosevelt was worried about both international threats and domestic concerns, and he called for the establishment of a centralized intelligence system. In July 1941, Roosevelt asked William J. Donovan to serve as the head of a new executive branch department, known first as the Coordinator of Information and eventually developing into the Office of Strategic Services.

As head of OSS, Donovan was charged with revolutionizing the intelligence efforts of the United States. He consulted with British allies who worked with British intelligence agency MI-6, which was at that point the leading intelligence agency in the world. With their help, OSS became the filter through which all intelligence—domestic and international—was appraised and shared with the president and other policymakers. In 1942, Donovan and his team of several hundred also carried out international missions to gather better, more crucial information about Axis activities and coordinated covert operations behind enemy lines. By 1944, the office that began with just 600 employees had grown to include 13,000, including 7,500 serving overseas, and a budget of close to $43 million per year.[2]

## The Central Intelligence Agency

While the OSS was able to quickly establish a sprawling intelligence network, it was never meant to be permanent, and with the end of World War II President Harry Truman called for Donovan to dismantle the agency. He was given just ten days to do so, moving the analysis function of OSS into the State Department and handing off international posts to a smaller organization called the Strategic Services Unit. But in early 1946,

President Truman and Congress established a new intelligence organization, called the Central Intelligence Group, which was given oversight of what had been the SSU's posts. In 1947, as CIG's duties grew to include espionage and covert operations, it was moved from the State Department's oversight to its own independent department. That department was renamed the Central Intelligence Agency.

The National Security Act of 1947 formally established the CIA, and tasked it to: "(1) advise the National Security Council (NSC) on matters related to national security; (2) make recommendations to the NSC regarding the coordination of intelligence activities of the Departments; (3) correlate and evaluate intelligence and provide for its appropriate dissemination and (4) 'perform such other functions...as the NSC will from time to time direct...'"[3] In 1949, President Truman also gave the CIA permission to fund covert operations and actions that deviated from standard governmental practices, something that would become a calling card of the agency for decades to come.

## The Cold War

By the early 1950s, the CIA was carrying out operations around the world and serving all branches of government by providing analysis related to efforts like the Korean War. It quickly grew into a massive, crucial part of the government. But the power of the CIA would be most clear as the 1950s continued and the post-war tension between the United States and the Soviet Union became more and more volatile. The Cold War was a rivalry of sorts between the two world powers, carried out primarily through proxy wars around the world and an arms race that saw both countries rushing to accumulate weapons of mass destruction. Secrecy and intrigue became the norms of the day, with both sides spying on one another in attempts to gain the upper hand.

Allen Dulles was the first civilian director of the CIA and was responsible for many of the changes that helped modernize the agency.

The CIA, in other words, played a large role in the Cold War. In addition to carrying out missions to spy on the Soviet Union and recruiting insiders to provide critical intelligence (something the Soviet Union did in the United States as well), the CIA carried out missions to depose governments thought to be sympathetic to the Soviets. The CIA organized failed missions like the Bay of Pigs, monitored developments in countries that could fall under Communist influence, and laid the foundation for conflicts like the Vietnam War. The CIA also established cultural efforts to counter Communism and Soviet influence, supporting dissident writers and funding arts publications like *The Paris Review* to spread American culture around the world. At home, the CIA was involved in experiments aimed at finding a special weapon

## ALLEN DULLES

In the mid-twentieth century, few had the influence over international affairs that the Dulles brothers did. John Foster Dulles and Allen Dulles were brought into power with the election of Dwight Eisenhower in 1952; the former was made secretary of state, while the latter became the first civilian director of the CIA, a position he would hold until 1961. Allen Dulles had previously worked with OSS and worked as deputy director of plans under the CIG. As director of central intelligence, Dulles oversaw Operation Ajax, which orchestrated a coup in Iran, and a coup in Guatemala. He was also instrumental in the Bay of Pigs invasion, one of the failures of the Kennedy administration. These early operations set the tone for the CIA's most well-known work—working against governments that were seen as hostile to US interests. But Dulles was forced to resign in 1961, following the Bay of Pigs, due to methods that were highly criticized.

against the Soviets, such as the MK-Ultra experiments that tested the mind-control potential of drugs like LSD.

## The CIA Today

When the Cold War ended with the fall of the Soviet Union in the early 1990s, the CIA's efforts focused primarily on the Middle East, an area that had been a hotbed of Cold War activity. But after the Soviet Union collapsed, terrorist cells began emerging in the region, sometimes made up of the very same insurgents that the CIA had trained to fight against Communist and Soviet forces. Particularly in Afghanistan, where the Mujahideen had been trained under the leadership of the CIA to fight against Soviet occupying forces, groups like al-Qaeda and the Taliban emerged and countered growing US influence by taking over the country. CIA involvement in the region grew with the First Gulf War in the mid-1990s and the emergence of the global war on terrorism in the early 2000s.

In more recent years, the CIA has come under attack for a lack of transparency and practices that many feel are unethical, including extraordinary rendition and possible surveillance of US citizens. The use of torture, or enhanced interrogation, at what are known as "black sites" has also been a cause for concern. Many in government and in the public worry that the CIA has become too difficult to provide oversight of and hold accountable for actions that violate norms and laws.

Over the course of several decades, the CIA grew from a small team of a few hundred people to a force capable of toppling governments. With that power has come significant scrutiny, cultural influence, and many controversies. But the CIA has proven over time that it can adapt quickly to changing world events, and it has been instrumental in the way the United States understands its place in the world.

CHAPTER 2

# THE DUTIES OF THE CIA

The Central Intelligence Agency is responsible for collecting, analyzing, and sharing information about a range of issues and subjects. Due to the international focus of the CIA, however, those tasks are carried out in a variety of interesting ways. What's more, the CIA also carries out missions and other activities in support of both its own and other departments' objectives, particularly the military. While it may not seem like a law enforcement agency, the CIA's operations actually connect with traditional law enforcement in unexpected ways.

## Gathering Intelligence

One of the reasons the OSS and eventually the CIA was founded was to address what President Roosevelt and others saw as an inadequate system to gather intelligence, which has remained one of the CIA's core functions ever since. Intelligence, however, doesn't mean simply facts

# THE DUTIES OF THE CIA

While the spies get all the glory, a lot of the work the CIA is responsible for is done by analysts and experts who work out of ordinary offices.

# INSIDE THE CIA

CIA agents often have to interrogate people, just like cops do, after a crime is committed. The only difference is that the CIA works to solve international crimes, not local crimes.

or figures. It refers to raw information, like audio or video recordings, foreign news reports, pictures, intercepted communications, snippets of information gathered from reports, or conversations that are later transcribed. This raw information can be incomplete, such as details about movements of a person of interest, or thorough, such as a video recording of an action taking place.

This information can also be collected in various ways. Monitoring specific people, such as the leadership of other countries suspected of taking part in terrorist funding, is one way the CIA is able to understand how networks operate. Spies or double agents are another, allowing the CIA to have access to behind-closed-door meetings and receive after-the-fact reports on what goes on in private. Drones can be useful means to gather imagery that can confirm large scale construction of, for example, nuclear facilities or military exercises. Bugging—or secretly installing recording devices—of spaces where meetings or events might take place, such as embassies, is a tactic that is both popular in fiction and used in real life. It is important to note that the CIA is not alone in using tactics like bugging and espionage; these are common practices among the world's intelligence agencies and have been for decades.

But some of the CIA's methods have been controversial, more so than spying or other common tactics. Enhanced interrogation, or the use of torture methods to force someone in detention to answer questions, is a heavily debated tactic in the United States. The CIA has been responsible for using these methods against people who are held without charge, often on possible links to terrorist organizations. But enhanced interrogation has been found to be ineffective; experts claim that those being interrogated will often give information that is false or confess to crimes they did not commit in order to make the torture, which can include waterboarding or held stress positions, stop. That these methods are often used at black sites off US territory, where it can be difficult to monitor or hold accountable those who authorize or carry out such actions, adds another layer of secrecy to an already obscured process.

## Analysis and Dissemination

Once the intelligence has been gathered, the CIA is responsible for analyzing it. Since the information it receives is often raw—or without context and explanation—it has to establish what it means, why it is important, and whether or not it requires action. In some cases, intelligence may not actually be helpful, or in other cases what appears to be useless could be helpful in the future. This is why analysis is such an important part of the process; it helps place intelligence within the framework of

### WORKING IN INTELLIGENCE

Careers with the CIA range from gathering intelligence to helping ensure the safety of CIA buildings. In order to qualify for a job at the CIA, it is important that a candidate be high achieving and has special skills, such as foreign language skills or specialized knowledge. The recruitment process is long and complicated, and it can involve tests. All jobs with the CIA are sorted into categories based on primary duties: analysis, clandestine, STEM, enterprise and support, and foreign language. These categories give us a sense of what kinds of jobs are available; jobs that fall under "analysis" include the gathering and analysis of intelligence, while jobs in "support" include managing facilities. "Foreign language" includes both teachers of languages and those with expert knowledge of language, while STEM focuses on technology. Clandestine, meanwhile, focuses on what we all think of when we think of the CIA: espionage.[1]

what we know, moving forward our understanding of events that take place around the world.

The CIA works with staff experts to analyze data relating to subjects around the world. Language experts are responsible for translating documents, including newspapers from around the world, which can help understand local context and developments on a micro scale, while subject matter experts, such as those with expertise on specific political situations, help place intelligence within the context of political hierarchy. It may seem mundane to question where particular members of a ruling class sit during a public event, but that kind of information can tell the CIA a lot about tensions within a government, who is likely gaining power, and who might even succeed the current leadership.

Once the intelligence has been analyzed, experts have to decide how best to share this information with the rest of the government. In some cases, in-depth reports that survey a wide-ranging issue are the best, providing highly detailed analysis of each development. But sometimes, as with pressing issues that develop quickly, it is more important to get the most critical information to leadership as soon as possible.

One of the ways the CIA provides information to leadership is through the president's daily briefing. This top-secret document is prepared with contributions from a number of intelligence agencies, including the FBI and the National Security Agency, as well as the CIA. The document includes information on threats, operations, developments of interest, and other analysis needed to make decisions or understand a number of situations around the globe and in the United States. Along with the president, the briefing is given to some high-ranking leadership within the government. Following a presidential election, the incoming president is provided with the briefing, as well, to ensure he or she is brought up to speed on the most important issues facing the country.

# INSIDE THE CIA

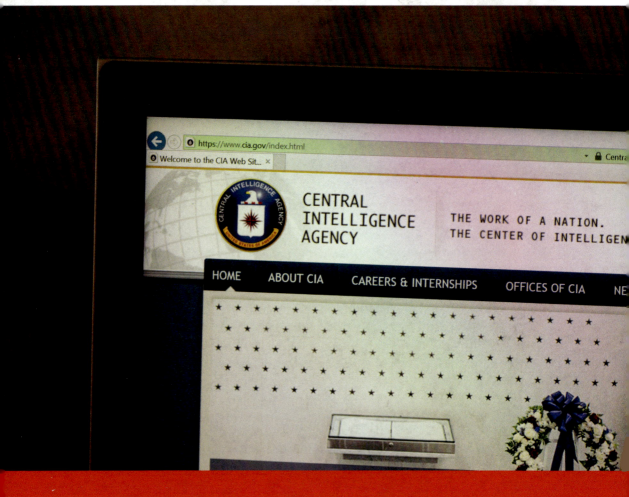

People can apply for jobs at the CIA just like they apply for any regular job, including by applying online. But getting the job is much harder and involves many security checks and months of training.

## Law Enforcement

The CIA also plays a role in supporting law enforcement in the United States, if not quite a direct one. The role of the CIA is largely investigative, and it has no authority to make arrests or carry out other police duties.

The only thing the CIA does domestically is share information gathered from a variety of sources with agencies and leaders. It then goes on to use that information to make decisions and take action.

So how does that support law enforcement? The CIA monitors potential threats that could take place on US soil but originate overseas, such as terrorist organizations that operate outside the country. It also plays a part in monitoring drug cartels, which could pose a threat to US citizens overseas or domestically. Information shared with organizations like the FBI or the Drug Enforcement Adminstration (DEA) can be critical for those organizations' efforts to counter threats.

CHAPTER 3

# THE CIA OVERSEAS

CIA operations in the United States are largely limited to analysis and dissemination, with the bulk of what we would consider action taking place outside of the country. Internationally, the CIA gathers intelligence, carries out operations, and cultivates relationships with intelligence agencies in allied countries. This work is what makes the CIA such an integral part of our government—it helps us understand not only our place in the world, but the possible changes looming on the horizon.

## Why International?

The CIA gathers and works with international intelligence—but why? The answer is fairly simple: The US intelligence community was formulated around the idea that the CIA operates within the sphere of international interests, while other agencies, such as the FBI, manage domestic intelligence gathering.[1] In part, this is because of their duties; the FBI serves

## THE CIA OVERSEAS

While the CIA is focused on international incidents, it often works with its stateside counterparts at the FBI and Homeland Security, as it did when President George W. Bush called for a joint operations center after 9/11.

as law enforcement in the United States, while the CIA doesn't. But it also speaks to the way the CIA developed, which was out of a wartime agency with posts around the world.

The international focus of the CIA is also a part of why it is so important; it employs some of the most specialized experts on international

INSIDE THE CIA

The CIA also works closely with its foreign counterparts. Here, US intelligence leaders are shown with their German counterparts after signing an agreement to share information.

affairs and uses that expertise to maintain up-to-date understanding of rapidly changing and long-term situations around the world. Consolidating the study of international intelligence allows the CIA to be the foremost expert on what would otherwise be a range of disparate issues, from terrorism to regime change to democratic institutions from South America to Asia.

## Intelligence Cooperation

The CIA doesn't always work alone. In fact, cooperation with international allies is a key way the CIA is able to gather information and intelligence. The British intelligence community, such as the agency MI-6, has been an ally to the US intelligence community since the founding of OSS, which the British helped establish. Other agencies, such as Israel's Mossad, have also been known to partner and cooperate with the CIA in gathering and sharing intelligence, as well as analysis.

Cooperation among intelligence agencies is complicated. Coordinated efforts can allow intelligence agencies to share information with one another, provide additional information, or even plan and carry out missions together. But there are limits to how much information an agency wants another country to have about its processes or what it knows. Depending on the country, a change in leadership can create tension that would make any deep knowledge a liability. What's more, sometimes intelligence agencies of allied countries spy on one another, such as a 1993 CIA operation in France that sought to gain information about upcoming economic negotiations.

Even with the tensions that come with spies working together, cooperation among allies is important. It allows all allied agencies to focus where they need to and benefit from different focuses carried out by other agencies, while also ensuring the kind of expertise that can only be gained from those who have lived and worked within a specific context. Through allies, the CIA is able to get better, smarter information and analysis, which allows the agency to better fulfill its mission.

## International Operations

Overseas posts are called stations—such as the Paris Station or the Tehran Station—and serve as the main base of operations for the CIA agents assigned to a particular area. The station takes direction from CIA headquarters in the United States and may coordinate with the embassy or consulate when needed, such as on missions that might endanger State Department staff. Stations can also be founded to address specific needs, such as the Bin Laden Issue Station, which began monitoring al-Qaeda in the late 1990s.

Stations are responsible for overseeing the gathering of intelligence on the ground. There are several ways stations go about doing so. Human intelligence, or HUMINT, is the use of espionage or human contacts; signal intelligence, or SIGNIT, is the interception of communications; imagery intelligence, or IMINT, is the use of usually overhead imagery; and financial intelligence, or FININT, is the tracking of bank records and financial transactions. All of this information is then used by analysts to provide updates to government officials.

## Covert Operations

Intelligence gathering is just one part of the CIA presence overseas; it also takes action when directed to by leadership, often in covert operations. Covert operations, which are planned and carried out by the Special Activities Division of the Directorate of Operations, can take many forms, such as coups or extraordinary renditions, a form of forcible removal from

## THE CIA OVERSEAS

### OPERATION AJAX

In August, 1953, the CIA carried out its first covert operation—a coup against the elected Iranian prime minister, Mohammed Mossadegh. Mossadegh was a popular politician who led the Communist National Front, a party that in the early 1950s had gained significant power due to British influence and exploitation of Iranian oil, which left many Iranians working in dangerous conditions and seeing little financial benefit. As prime minister, Mossadegh nationalized the oil refineries and kicked out the British, setting off an international crisis. In response, the British, with the CIA, organized a coup against Mossadegh. Over the course of two weeks, CIA operatives led by Kermit Roosevelt organized street protests, the dismissal of Mossadegh, and arrests of his allies, forcing him out of office and putting in his place a US-backed military leader. In the years to come, the Shah of Iran would tighten his hold on power, using secret police to spread fear and target dissidents until 1979, when the Islamic Revolution toppled his government.

one country to another in order to carry out interrogation. The CIA has also been behind assassination attempts, including numerous attempts on Cuban leader Fidel Castro. As part of the global war on terror, the CIA has also been given the power to carry out targeted assassinations against those believed to be high-ranking terrorists. Former president Barack Obama banned it from using drones to do so; however, President Donald Trump reversed that order, allowing the CIA to use unmanned aircraft to carry out airstrikes against potential terrorist targets.

The nature of covert operations varies. Some, such as coups, involve carefully planned actions and coordination between many different stakeholders. Others, like secretive propaganda efforts, might include fewer participants and lower budgets, although they are still carefully

During the Cold War, under President Ronald Reagan, the CIA expanded its covert operations and helped arm the Afghan mujahideen in their war against the Soviet Union.

planned to ensure efficiency. What makes a covert operation different from other overt operations is the legal framework in which they take place and the secrecy with which they are carried out. The CIA is the only agency empowered to carry out such missions, unless the president designates another agency to do so and Congress is officially informed. President Ronald Reagan also made it legal via executive order for the government to deny knowledge of these operations, even though all covert operations must be signed off on by the president and are monitored by committees in Congress.

Covert operations are by far one of the most well-known facets of CIA work, but they make up a small part of the analysis and intelligence sharing that the agency carries out. What's more, covert operations have made the CIA a force for, in many cases, negative change around the world. Today, leadership often cites the CIA and the work the agency has done around the world when cracking down on dissidents or protests, arresting civilians, or otherwise hindering free political expression. This is because in countries from Asia to South America, the CIA has played a role in key moments of political upheaval, sometimes resulting in dictatorships or undue suffering.

CHAPTER 4

# CONTROVERSIES OF THE CIA

The CIA is an important part of our government, gathering and analyzing intelligence that is critical to ensuring national security. But as with any powerful organization, the CIA is not without long-standing issues and controversies. Given the nature of the CIA's work, those issues are often linked to the nature of democracy and the ways in which a powerful state can overstep in the name of defending interests abroad.

## Lack of Transparency and Accountability

By its nature, the CIA is a secretive organization that does not share a great deal of its work with the public after an operation. If reports are released, they are redacted heavily to maintain the safety of those involved or ensure processes remain confidential. But the CIA is still under the oversight of the president and Congress, meaning that there

When agencies like the CIA face controversy, their leaders are often brought before Congress to testify about what went wrong and how it can be fixed.

is some expectation of disclosure. However, many fear that the CIA is not as forthcoming with information as it could or should be and that this lack of transparency is a dangerous feature of an organization with the ability to carry out targeted strikes or covert operations.

Transparency is an important part of democracy—it helps us know what the government is doing in our name as citizens. The CIA, however, has a black budget, which means that Congress approves an amount for each fiscal year but does not know how the money will be spent. Tens of billions of dollars are allocated to the CIA each year, a number that often rises significantly from year to year, but the CIA is not required to make public how that money is spent, which some fear makes the organization's operations too secretive. It also makes it difficult to hold the agency accountable, as we often only learn about operations and actions after the fact—and sometimes years later.

## DOMESTIC SURVEILLANCE

The CIA is responsible for international operations and surveillance, including intelligence-gathering methods like espionage. Traditionally, it is not thought of as responsible for domestic surveillance, which is overseen by the FBI and other agencies charged with tasks that center on US territory. But domestic surveillance has always been part of the CIA story, often with controversial results. A sprawling investigation in 1975 called the Church Committee found that between the 1950s and 1970s, the CIA had taken part in domestic surveillance that included opening letters and that hundreds of thousands of Americans were in a CIA surveillance database. In 2003, President George W. Bush announced the opening of the Terrorist Threat Integration Center, which coordinates efforts across law enforcement to monitor potential terrorist threats. In 2013, Edward Snowden revealed that the CIA was one part of the intelligence community that was carrying out surveillance of domestic citizens, which led to significant outcry. These allegations raise questions about privacy, government overreach, and accountability in the age of the internet, where many citizens give up personal data for access to websites.

There have also been recent controversies regarding how the CIA submits to watchdog groups and whether or not the organization is being forthcoming with necessary information. Although not required by law to send data to government watchdog groups for classified operations, the CIA has argued that even unclassified operations contain information that would be detrimental to its mission and the safety of the country. But some politicians and advocates aren't so sure and have called for an overhaul of how the CIA handles information given to the public in an attempt to make holding the agency accountable a little easier.

## Enhanced Interrogation

In recent years, one of the most significant and recurring controversies surrounding the CIA is the use of enhanced interrogation, a technique of questioning that some feel amounts to torture. These techniques involve nonfatal tactics, such as waterboarding, to simulate danger in a way that makes those being questioned provide information. But while that might sound straight forward, enhanced interrogation is far more complex, both in terms of ethics and efficiency.

Enhanced interrogation is called by supporters one of the most efficient and effective ways to get potential terrorists to share information critical to national security. But opponents say that it is actually ineffective and that those being questioned have been found to give false information more often than accurate information. There are also concerns about the accuracy of allegations of terrorist activity when it comes to those being questioned; there have been cases of individuals being arrested on very little evidence, only to learn later—and in some cases much later—that they were not involved in terrorist activities. What's more, opponents argue that in some cases nonfatal tactics can be used too heavily and can do lasting physical damage to those being questioned or even result in their deaths.

The CIA carries out enhanced interrogation at sites around the world, but it is most closely associated with black sites, which are off US territory and have limited oversight. This makes it all the more important that the safety and effectiveness of enhanced interrogation be debated among leaders and voters and that there be a way the CIA can be held accountable when these tactics are used incorrectly or with a person wrongfully accused of terrorist activity. The fact that little has been done to ensure that the system works in a way that is ethical, safe, and with a guarantee of due process for those accused has made opponents concerned that the CIA remains not only lacking in transparency, but also a poor reflection of US values.

## International Impact

Another long-standing concern about the CIA is its overall international impact, particularly on the development of democratic politics in foreign countries. The CIA has been involved, by its own admission, in coups against elected leadership in countries around the world, and its work to unseat those governments has often lead to the development of more harsh, authoritarian regimes—sometimes with US backing and CIA assistance. This can cause years of struggle to establish democratic norms and often puts in danger dissidents and opposition political parties. Rather than making the world a more democratic place, which is one of the United States' stated values in regards to foreign policy, the CIA has been behind or taken part in actions that undermine freedom and sometimes lead to prolonged conflict.

This potential to cause unrest has made the CIA legendary around the world and has had unsettling consequences. In Afghanistan, CIA- and

## CONTROVERSIES OF THE CIA

While the CIA is supposed to only do international intelligence work, the infamous Edward Snowden leaks of 2013 showed that the CIA, like the NSA, was also gathering intelligence at home in America.

Among the many methods of intelligence gathering the CIA uses is the polygraph, or lie detector, which uses a person's pulse rate to determine if they are telling the truth.

US-backed militants worked to force Soviet forces from the country but eventually became the Taliban and al-Qaeda, groups against which the United States has since fought against. In South America, US-backed dictatorships have given rise to civil war, such as in Peru. And the reach of the CIA's influence isn't limited to actions it takes; in countries where the CIA has a history of intervention and those where it does not, leadership leans on the threat of CIA-backed espionage and coups to justify cracking down on civilians and opponents, a dangerous use of the legacy of unrest the agency has left behind but for which it is rarely held accountable.

CHAPTER 5

# THE FUTURE OF THE CIA

Since the founding of the OSS in 1942, US intelligence has been on the cutting edge of gathering and sharing critical information about national and international security. But it has also been a source of concern among leaders and activists around the world, creating precedents for international intervention that have had disastrous consequences alongside those that have ensured the safety of US interests. What does the twenty-first century hold for this storied agency?

## The Cyber Age

In 2015, the CIA opened a groundbreaking new department: the Directorate of Digital Innovation.[1] The creation of this department says a great deal about where the CIA is heading in coming decades, as technology and computers become even more integral to how people engage in their everyday lives and share information about themselves and the world

In 2018, Gina Haspel was confirmed as the director of the CIA, making her the first woman to lead the famous spy agency.

around them. The DDI is charged with ensuring agents are trained in cyber strategies of intelligence work and counterintelligence work and making sure that information about cyber threats is shared efficiently and effectively across the agency. It's a shift that makes sense, as the internet has changed the way people around the world communicate and the way governments work against one another—in fact, the DDI was founded after a large-scale hack of the government's Office of Personnel Management.

Hacking by foreign governments has emerged since 2015 as a significant threat to national security. Hostile governments are able to access anything from election systems to the electrical grid if they are able to find a weakness. At the same time, groups like ISIS have adapted to use social media, rather than traditional communication methods, to recruit from anywhere around the globe. It is therefore crucial for intelligence professionals to understand how to navigate this cyber universe—and how to share that information as quickly as possible, as everything online moves at a speed

## ENCOURAGING ACCOUNTABILITY

If there is one thorn in the side of the CIA, it remains the lack of transparency and accountability that has dogged the agency for decades. While a level of secrecy is important for safety, it is equally important that the public—in the United States and around the world—knows that the CIA is an ethical agency working within a framework to which it will be held accountable, should it violate laws. Finding ways to reform the agency in a way that encourages accountability will not only heal some of the wounds left by the CIA over the years but will show a way for intelligence to be ethical and truly global in the twenty-first century.

# INSIDE THE CIA

In 2015, the CIA added a Directorate of Digital Innovation to make sure its agents are properly trained to deal with the many new threats that come from the internet.

traditional threats might not. Shifting focus toward those threats, while maintaining traditional means of HUMINT and other intelligence gathering, will ensure the CIA remains one step ahead of potential dangers.

## Politics and Intelligence

The CIA is a crucial part of our governmental operations—but things aren't always friendly between administrations and the agency. In fact, many presidents have clashed with the intelligence community or shown hostility to relying on its expertise, dating back to the Truman administration's hesitancy to even create a permanent, peace-time intelligence agency in the wake of World War II. But presidents being hostile to the

The future of the CIA will be determined by its leaders and the administrations they work with. Director Haspel and President Trump will shape the agency for years to come.

intelligence community can be dangerous, particularly if it causes them to overlook potential threats that otherwise need attention. What's more, if an administration doesn't provide support to the CIA, the organization could stagnate under neglect, becoming less effective.

The opposite dynamic—in which the CIA and the administration work hand in hand—can also be dangerous. The CIA has significant power and authority, and in the past that has been turned toward US citizens. Doing so undermines its mission and poses questions about overreach, both by the CIA and the administration it is serving at any given time. The CIA must remain an independent body with significant oversight, not a tool for partisan aims.

# CHAPTER NOTES

## Chapter 1. A History of the CIA

1. "COI Came First," CIA.gov, https://www.cia.gov/library/publications/intelligence-history/oss/art02.htm.
2. "History of the CIA," CIA.gov, https://www.cia.gov/about-cia/history-of-the-cia.
3. Ibid.

## Chapter 2. The Duties of the CIA

1. "Career Opportunities," CIA.gov, https://www.cia.gov/careers/opportunities.

## Chapter 3. The CIA Overseas

1. Robert Valencia, "CIA, FBI, NSA, DIA: What's the Difference, and What Does Each Do?" Mic.com, February 17, 2017, https://mic.com/articles/168921/cia-fbi-nsa-dia-what-s-the-difference-and-what-does-each-do#.of0hbUTRY.

## Chapter 5. The Future of the CIA

1. Suzanne Kelly, "The CIA's Officer of the Future," The Cipher Brief, May 28, 2017, https://www.thecipherbrief.com/column_article/best-of-the-cias-officer-of-the-future-2.

# GLOSSARY

**black site** A location that is unacknowledged and top secret and is often used for interrogation.

**Central Intelligence Agency** The United States' foremost intelligence organization, with a focus on international targets.

**Cold War** An indirect conflict between the United States and the Soviet Union that took place between the late 1940s and early 1990s.

**coup** The intentional planning and carrying out of the overthrow of a government.

**double agent** Someone who claims to work for one country while actually working for another and using access to gain classified or privileged information.

**enhanced interrogation** A method of questioning that uses nonfatal tactics, including forms of torture, to force someone to give up information.

**espionage** Spying or otherwise using covert means to gain information.

**extraordinary rendition** The movement of an individual from one country to another country, usually where regulations on interrogation are less strict, for questioning.

**intelligence** Information used by organizations like the CIA to determine threats, changes in situations around the world, or other developments.

**Mujahideen** A group of Afghan insurgents who fought against Soviet forces in the 1970s and 1980s, with CIA and US backing.

## GLOSSARY

**Office of Strategic Services** The World War II–era forerunner to the CIA.

**proxy war** A conflict in which both sides are supported by other countries, making it a fight between those countries as well.

**transparency** Voluntary sharing of information with the public or with a watchdog group to ensure all actions and operations are understood.

**unethical** Morally wrong.

# FURTHER READING

## Books

Andrew, Christopher. *The Secret World: A History of Intelligence.* New Haven, CT: Yale University Press, 2018.

Hurt, Avery Elizabeth. *Code Breakers and Spies of the Cold War.* New York, NY: Cavendish Square Publishing, 2019.

Pender, Lionel. *The Spy Game: International and Military Intelligence.* New York, NY: Rosen Publishing, 2017.

## Websites

**Central Intelligence Agency**
www.cia.gov
The main website for the CIA, it offers the story and history of the Agency, job listings, and recently released information from the Agency's archives.

**CIA on YouTube**
www.youtube.com/user/ciagov
The CIA's official YouTube account features videos created by the agency to show off its officers and technology and to tell stories about the work they do to protect Americans around the world.

**New York Times**
www.nytimes.com/topic/organization/central-intelligence-agency
The newspaper's archives have news stories about the CIA, including stories about its history and many controversies.

# INDEX

## A
Afghanistan, 13, 34–36
al-Qaeda, 13, 26, 36
assassinations, 27

## B
Bay of Pigs, 12
black sites, 13, 18, 34
Bush, George W., 32

## C
Castro, Fidel, 27
Central Intelligence Agency (CIA)
    controversies, 4, 13, 17, 30–36
    duties, 4, 5, 10, 14–21, 22, 32
    failed missions, 12
    founding/history of, 4–5, 7–13, 14
    future of, 37–42
    overseas, 22–29
    power of, 13
    today, 13
    working for the, 18
Central Intelligence Group (CIG), 10, 12
Cold War, 5, 7, 10–13
Communism, 12, 13, 27
coups, 5, 12, 26, 27, 34, 36
covert operations, 9, 10, 26–29
Cuba, 12, 27
cyber threats, 39–41

## D
Directorate of Digital Innovation (DDI), 37–39
domestic surveillance, 32
Donovan, William J., 9
drones, 17, 27
Dulles, Allen, 12
Dulles, John Foster, 12

## E
Eisenhower, Dwight, 12
enhanced interrogation, 5, 13, 17–18, 33–34
espionage, 4, 7, 10, 17, 18, 26, 32, 36
extraordinary rendition, 13, 26

## F
Federal Bureau of Investigation (FBI), 4, 8, 19, 22–23, 32

## G
Great Britain, 9, 25, 27
    intelligence agencies, 9, 25

## H
hacking, computer, 39

## I
intelligence cooperation, 25–26
intelligence gathering, 4, 6, 7–9, 10, 12, 14–18, 22, 26, 32, 37
   analysis and dissemination of information, 18–19, 22, 29
international impact, 34–36
international operations, 26
Iran, 12, 27
ISIS, 39

## L
law enforcement, 6, 14, 20–21, 23

## M
military, 7–8, 14
Mossad, 25
Mossadegh, Mohammed, 27
Mujahideen, 13
Murphy, Robert, 8

## N
National Security Act, 10
National Security Agency, 19

## O
Obama, Barack, 27

Office of Strategic Services (OSS), 4, 7–9, 12, 14, 25, 37
Operation Ajax, 12, 27

## P
politics and intelligence, 41–42
president's daily briefing, 19

## R
Reagan, Ronald, 29
Roosevelt, Franklin, 4, 9, 14

## S
Snowden, Edward, 32
Soviet Union, 10–13, 36
State Department, 9, 10, 26
stations, 26
Strategic Services Unit, 9–10

## T
Taliban, 13, 36
terrorism, 13, 17, 21, 25, 27, 32, 34
torture, 5, 13, 17–18, 33–34
transparency and accountability, lack of, 5, 13, 30–33, 39
Truman, Harry, 9–10, 41
Trump, Donald, 27

## W
World War II, 4, 7, 9, 41